MW01230974

Bridging the Gap Between Pain and Purpose

Yulanda Braxton

Bridging the Gap Between Pain and Purpose

Copyright © 2020 Yulanda Braxton

All rights reserved.

ISBN (Print Version): 979-8691606298

Cover Design: Shekinah Glory Publishing'

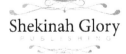

Shekinah Glory
PUBLISHING

www.shekinahglorypublishing.org

(936) 314-7458

Dedication

I dedicate this book to my heavenly Father.

Thank you, God, for sending your angel to let me know that I must not be offended by anyone or anything. This book has freed me, and I pray that other men and women will find freedom from their painful pasts to fulfill their God given purpose.

Acknowledgements

To **Mrs. Irma Bundage**, my high school counselor, you helped me more than you would ever know during my teenage years.

To **Novie Lefluer**, my God Sister, thank you for always being there for me and inspiring me to write this book.

To my brothers, **Joel Brown** and **Kotto Brown**, thank you for loving me unconditionally.

To my **Mom and Dad**, thank you for all you did for us. Love you both.

Lastly, to my husband **Rogers Braxton**. I want to thank you for showing me how a woman deserves to be loved and showing me what a husband is. I love you much!

Table of Contents

Introduction

Pain and purpose! I've been told that it's impossible to have one without the other. Who in there right mind would want to associate the gruesome emotional, mental, spiritual, and physical elements of pain with the daily grind of trying to fulfill purpose? Well, I hate to be the bearer of bad news, but in order to evolve into the purpose driven man or woman that God created you to be, pain will be the driving force.

Pain will serve as an invisible motivator that will cheer you on towards your predestined future. Don't feel bad because the pain doesn't last forever, but it does come in many different forms. This may be the hardest part to accept. We never know from day to day what we will experience. We never know what trials, tribulations, or hardships will come to test, train, and prepare us for our next. You are probably saying "next what" well your next level or season.

We were not created to stay stuck in the same place year after year. Even the world is designed to shift with the seasons. God created winter, spring, summer, and fall. Our lives are designed to shift in seasons, but many times we choose to stay stuck in a particular season because it appears to be more comfortable. Well, it may appear to be comfortable, but imagine, shifting to spring, but still wearing a fur coat like its winter. First, you will burn up and secondly you will look weird and out of place.

We walk around in life trying to find our place. Searching for that "thing" designed to make us feel whole, complete, successful, and loved. If you have found the secret to total success without pain please share it with me, but realistically there is no secret. It is all about process. Yes, I know we don't like that word. I don't like it either because it requires work.

You and I must be willing to "Bridge the Gap Between Our Pain and Our Purpose!" There are two strategic definitions for "bridge" I would like to address. The first is a structure carrying a pathway or roadway over a depression or obstacle. The second is a time, place, or means of connection or transition. How many obstacles have you either had or may be experiencing at this moment? Have you found yourself in a depressed state of being? If you answered yes, then it's time to build a bridge that will carry you over the obstacles of life and the seasons of depression and oppression that have attempted to keep you stuck.

It is time for your life to transition from one place to another, from one season to another, from one level to another. This sounds complicated, but change is always difficult at first. The more steps you take, the easier each step will become. Like I said, it's a process that is neither easy nor cheap. Process will come at a great cost. The question is how much are you willing to pay? How much is it worth to transition from brokenness to wholeness?

Just think about how much its costing you now if anything. You could be in a place where you are comfortably, uncomfortable. This means you have settled and therefore you are uncomfortable, but you have figured out how to make it work. No ma'am and No sir! You picked up this book for a reason. If you wanted to support me, I deeply appreciate the gesture, but this is about you. This is about you making the connection between your pain and your purpose.

This is about giving your pain a voice and giving attention to your purpose. This is your time and you must take advantage before you find yourself going around that mountain one more time. I have been there in my life and believe me it doesn't feel good. I have always had the best intentions; yet they didn't go the way I planned them in my head. Therefore, I have found myself in some sticky situations because I was thinking with my emotions and not my heart. My heart and my intuition were screaming no, but that emotional dysfunction fell for the okie doke every time.

I should be a poster child for dysfunctional relationships. I have always given the other person the benefit of the doubt, but where were my benefits? Did that strike a nerve? I hope so, because it struck one with me when I finally realized that I was making me irrelevant, when I should have been first after God. I can't cry over spoiled milk, and neither can you, but we can take a hard look in the mirror, access the damage, and make the necessary adjustments.

Friends I had to adjust. I mean really and truly adjust, which started with acknowledging my truth. I had been lying to myself for a long time. I had a mask on that I didn't want to take off, but one day I reached "my enough is enough" point and I started building my bridge one brick at a time. You see I wanted to see the end results through my eyes, but only God knows the end from the beginning. You have to pick up your pieces of the puzzle and allow God to help you fit them with the right pieces. You can't go wrong with God. So, as I share the pieces of my story and how I have worked to "Bridge the Gap Between My Pain and My Purpose" I pray that you will be blessed by my transparency, strength, and hope for a better tomorrow.

Happy reading!

Chapter One
A Distorted Foundation

As children we are taught to dream big! We are told that the sky is the limit! The adults constantly preach that there is nothing we can't do if we put out minds to it! Blah, Blah, Blah! If you have heard one, you've heard them all. Well, its one thing to hear and its another to listen and believe. As children we are taught to be open and receptive to life. We are free to love, dream, and explore. We are conditioned to lean and depend on our parents for any and everything.

As we grow, the foundation for life that is laid by our parents should be solid, but what happens if and when the foundation begins to crack? What happens when the walls of love that were built to shelter, provide, and protect begin to cave in and one day come tumbling down? What happens when emotions begin to swell up and suddenly things such as trust and reliability begin to explode? This might not be your story, but it is definitely mine.

My parents met at a funeral in Houston, Texas where they started dating, got married, and then I was conceived. I was born in Houston, but raised in Baytown, Texas. I am the oldest of two brothers who are only a year apart. I love my brothers, but I must admit that I enjoyed being the only child for several years before my first brother was born.

I was a daddy's girl and I adored the attention that I received from my father. There was nothing I couldn't get from him. I enjoyed jumping in his lap after a long day of work and hugging his neck. I knew he loved and protected me, and I loved him to. As a child my life was perfect. We had what many might consider the family with the white picket fence, but one day the house didn't feel as cozy anymore.

After the birth of my first brother, my father wasn't as happy or approachable. He appeared to be agitated all the time and my mother started to change as well. She wasn't smiling like she used to. At the time I didn't have a clue as to what was going on. I wasn't sure if she was sick or tired, but I knew something wasn't right.

My parents tried to hide their issues, but I was always very observant.

Despite the changes in the home, I can recall so many candid childhood memories. My dad always sent me to school with fresh cut lemons. They were sour but I loved eating them. Throughout elementary school I was the tallest in my class. This caused me to stand out. Being tall was one thing, but my mother made matters worse when she combed my hair into several little plats. The kids teased me and gave me the name "spider woman."

Life for me during that time was somewhat bizarre to say the least. Aside from my mother's hair combing woes, she wasn't that good at dressing me either. I had this awful polyester outfit that not only itched, but it was extremely hot. The colors in the top resembled a peacock and during this time we didn't change clothes for PE, so I had to sweat and itch during and after class. Then there was my kindergarten picture day. I had on a brown overall dress with ponytails.

Man, those were the days and I'm so grateful I can dress myself today. That was torture, but outside of the 70's fashion disasters, there was something else on the horizon.

There was trouble in our home and as a child I felt it, but there was nothing I could do. Around the age of nine I recall taking a family portrait. Normally, the family portrait consists of the husband sitting next to his wife holding hands and the children standing behind them. The photographer says "cheese", and everyone smiles and appears to be one big happy family.

Well, on this particular day, we were there, and we appeared to be a family, but mama wasn't happy. She wasn't smiling at all. She didn't even pretend to smile. I noticed it, but again I was a child, what did I know. They say a picture is worth a thousand words. Our family portrait was speaking loud and clear.

Even though my mother wasn't happy, it never stopped her from being our mother. We were everything to her. She held on to us for dear life. Wherever she went we were tagging right behind. We were never at home. My father worked all the time, so it was never an issue for him.

Eventually bad got worse between my mother and father. It was so bad that my father left. This was devastating for me because no child wants to see their parents fight or not be in their lives. I loved my father even though he was changing right before my very eyes. I didn't feel like his little princess anymore. The bond we once had was slowly fading away. To be honest it hadn't faded, in my opinion it was gone.

One day I was standing outside playing in front of the house. At the time my father had a motorcycle and I could hear one coming up the street, so I stood there in anticipation waiting to see if it was him. From a distance I could see him coming. I was getting excited because I thought he was coming to visit. As he approached the house, I could see a woman on the bike with him. At that moment everything around me stood still and started to go in slow motion. The next thing I know I'm being egged by the woman on the bike.

Yes, you read that right! My father, the man who was responsible for me being in the earth passed by and allowed this woman to throw eggs not only at his child, but at the house he shared with his wife and children. Once I snapped out of the trance I was in due to shock, I could hear them laughing as they drove away. I never told anyone about this horrible experience. This was another traumatic event that I buried in the depths of my soul.

After my father left, he moved in with his mother who lived down the street. He wasn't paying the bills so eventually our lights were caught off for nonpayment. My mother had to drop her pride and walk down to my grandmother's house to beg my father to come home. He finally gave in and came back. I can't say I was excited because nothing was the same anymore. The tension in the house was so thick you could cut it with a knife.

Turns out my father had been abusing my mother, but we didn't know. This is why her smiles turned to frowns and she couldn't be still or peaceful at home. She was trying to escape the hidden pain and hide the secret tears that were constantly welling up in her heart, mind, body, and soul.

As humans we are not designed to withstand a lot of pressure. There is only so much abuse one person can take. My mother finally reached her point of no return. One day she was in the kitchen cooking a pot of spaghettis. As she stood over the pot, the dormant pain began to rise up on the inside of her and she simply said, "I can't do this anymore!"

A light flashed in the midst of her darkness and reminded her that she was in a place she could be delivered from. The cell door to the prison called her marriage opened and she was about to make her exit.

On this particular day, I was riding my bike with some friends. When I returned home, I walked into a yelling match between my parents. My mother snapped that day and made a choice to choose her. At the time I didn't understand the value in her choosing herself with three innocent children hanging in the balance, but now that I am an adult who has experienced her fair share of man hurt, I can say I understand. It doesn't negate the damage caused by her decision, but I get it.

When this first happened, I was numb. My mother left me and my brothers with our dad for almost two years. I could never truly describe how empty the house felt without her, plus the coldness from my father was unnerving. I can honestly say he did the best he could, but he wasn't mama. He didn't possess the nurturing, patient, gentle, and loving attitude that our mother had.

We were still required by law to be with our mother on weekends and holidays because my father filed child support on her. I honestly don't think she cared as long as she didn't have to deal with him and his abuse. I took on the responsibility of trying to mother and nurture my little brothers. I was growing up much faster than I wanted to.

Somewhere along the journey I think I checked out mentally, spiritually, and emotionally. I learned how to go with the flow. I was a walking zombie who developed a routine called survival. I learned how to survive as a child because the adults in my life made choices to suit them. Choices that didn't involve the betterment of me and my brothers, making for a very distorted family foundation.

Chapter Two

When Bad Gets Worse

W hen I think back to the days of my youth, I often find myself shaking my head. As a young girl I don't know how I was able to navigate through the trauma I was forced to experience as a result of my parents. I didn't ask for any of this, but dysfunction is the hand I was dealt. Unfortunately, I didn't ask to be born and I didn't have the option of picking parents. God chose them for me.

Life felt like a horrible trick was being played on me because no one in their right mind could consider my life normal. There was nothing normal about my life, but now that I am older, I realize there were other children dealing with hardships that were similar or worse than mine. Living with my dad and visiting with my mom was frustrating, but I learned to go with the flow.

My father was always on the prowl looking for a replacement mother to take care of me and my brothers. Therefore, he didn't have time to be a full time dad between work and women. Again, I get it! Men are different from women, but to be honest my father didn't even try to bond with us. I can recall one Christmas during my teenage years. My father put up the Christmas tree. As a teenager I'm not sure what I was expecting, but my father bought me a teddy bear like I was still a little girl.

I'm sure he felt like he had given me the world and I should be appreciative. It felt like he didn't put any thought or effort into the gift. Like he waited to the last minute to run to the store and grab something for the sake of not looking like an inconsiderate parent. Now, let me be clear these are my feelings. He could have been absolutely sincere, but no holiday would ever have the same meaning without my mother being there.

After my mother moved out, she went to live with a Caucasian woman named Sue. My father was very adamant about keeping his personal business a secret, which meant we were forbidden to tell my mother anything about my fathers' whereabouts or his lady friends. One day my mother called looking for my father because she needed to drop my brothers off. She reached out to me and I told her my father was out with his girlfriend.

When my father found out, he was livid. He sent my uncle and grandmother to get me from my friend's house. I hid in my friends' closet because I knew it wasn't going to be good for me. I hid until they left because if I was going to get beat, it was going to be on my terms and not his. I took a deep breath and made my way towards the house.

My father greeted me at the door and said, "If you come in this house, I am going to beat you!" I replied, "Then I'm not coming in the house because I don't feel like I deserve to be beat!" He replied, "Then you can't come in!"

I stood there in shock! I couldn't believe that I was being scolded for being a child and not fully understanding the madness between him and my mother. They were separated, therefore, why did it matter who he was with? She left him! He had the right to do whatever he wanted. In the midst of all this chaos, my mother pulled up and I was standing outside. She pretty much figured he was upset, so she dropped my brothers off and told me to get in the car.

This was another numbing moment in my life. I felt rejected and thrown away by a man who was supposed to protect me. This ping pong process I was experiencing at the hands of my parents was creating a wounded girl that would one day grow into a wounded woman.

My mother dropped me off at school the next morning and after school I rode the bus home to my dad's house. I had no idea what to expect. I wasn't sure if I was walking into the beating that I avoided the day before or not.

When my father walked in and saw me, he simply said he was angry, but we would work through it. He cooked dinner and we ate. Afterwards he asked me to clean the kitchen, which at that time I told him I wasn't staying, I was just coming to get my stuff.

This bit of information didn't sit well with him. He instructed me to only take the items my mother bought and nothing he paid for. I did exactly what he said. When I was finish packing, I went to my friend's house and called my mom.

My mother picked me up and we went on our way. Eventually my mom moved to Houston and we lived there during my seventh and eight grade year. My father and I didn't have a relationship at all during this time. There are no words to truly describe how this felt. I can understand him acting this way towards my mother, but not me. I was his only daughter. No young girl should have to navigate through life without the guidance and love of her father.

I really thought being with my mother would be better, but it wasn't, plus I missed my brothers. My mother became more like a girlfriend than a parent. Now that I am an adult, I somewhat understand the need to spread your wings and fly after being in a committed relationship with kids.

I had no comprehension of this as a child. I was flat out angry and didn't understand what she was doing. She was no longer the mother that I was accustomed to. There were days when we would hang out at Duessen Park with her girlfriends, just talking and laughing.

I was never fully able to be in a child's place because I was always around adults or in the midst of adult drama. I remember being around thirteen years old, when I met this guy named Carter. I had a pair of zipper jeans that were zipped from the front to the back. He had this look on his face like he had never saw anything like it before. We started talking and he actually confirmed that my fashion was something new for him. Despite my unusual sense of fashion Carter became my first boyfriend.

My mother was consumed with her life and living in her world; therefore, I was pretty much left to myself. She didn't hassle me about school and making good grades, so I wasn't motivated to do anything. What's the point if she wasn't going to be there to support me anyway? I went to school, but barely did any work. I did enough just to get by.

Eventually, I found myself lost in an array of male companionship. I can honestly say I wasn't having sex, but I was talking the boys ears off. This helped me to temporarily fill the voids in my life. During this time, I was so angry. I was living life in a whirlwind and wherever the whirlwind landed was fine with me.

I didn't have any ambition or drive. I was missing that part of my life where I was supposed to dream about my future. My future was looking really bleak because the crowd I was hanging with was into all kinds of stuff. I was following the crowd and doing what everyone else was doing, with the exception of having sex.

Thank God, I had enough sense not to cross that path. I don't know how I avoided it because I was doing everything else. If they said "jump" I didn't have to say how high, I just jumped. I wanted to go along to get along. Being rejected by my father was causing me to go over and beyond to be recognized by people who didn't even matter. Yet, I needed to be validated just that bad. I needed to be seen and I didn't care who saw me, as long as I received some form of recognition.

All of this acting out caused me to repeat the eighth grade twice. This was beyond embarrassing. I failed the eighth grade in Houston and eventually my mother and I moved back to Baytown.

Once the divorce was settled my mother received the house and got custody of my brothers. This was somewhat exciting because I was able to be near my brothers again, but this also meant having to face my father as well.

After being gone for almost two years I just knew my father would have worked past his issues with me. One day my father came to pick up the boys and my mother told me I had to go too. God knows I didn't want to go, but my mother was trying to force a relationship between us. Sad to say, but it didn't work. I packed my bag and waited for him to arrive. When he pulled up, he popped the trunk for us to put our bags in the car. I went to get in the car, and he said I couldn't go. Can you imagine the look on my face? Not that I wanted to go, but he could have announced this when he saw me standing at the door with my bags.

I said, "Okay, I will get my stuff out the trunk!" He replied, "No, you can get it when I bring them back!" He was really tripping! It felt like he intentionally waited for me to put my bag in the trunk to tell me I couldn't go in hopes that it would hurt me. He saw me walk to the car and had ample enough time to ask me where I was going or something.

When I think back, this truly crushed me. I wasn't a stranger, but he was treating me like one. I never tried to choose between him and my mother, it just happened because I didn't want to get a whipping. What child wants to get a beating? I know I didn't, especially for something petty. The cracks in my foundational family structure were getting bigger and bigger.

There was nothing really solid or pleasant going on in my life. Each day I found myself trying to figure out life through the mind of a teenager and that was dangerous. I couldn't figure out for the life of me why my father was so angry with me. He acted as if he had something to prove. Like he had a vendetta against me. Could it have been that I reminded him of my mother?

Well, to be honest he wasn't treating my brothers any better, but I believe he kept them due to the child support and nothing else. Whatever the true reason, I needed him in my life, but unfortunately, he couldn't work past his own personal issues.

Chapter Three
"Why Me, Lord?"

I 'm sure we've all had those moments when we said, "Why Me, Lord?" People that don't even know God on a personal level find themselves calling on Him during those tough times and rough patches in their lives. I was only a kid, but I knew enough to know that my life was rough. I didn't deserve the things I was experiencing at the hands of my father, but today I understand he couldn't do anymore for me, than what was done for him.

This is sad to say and I am not making excuses, but it's hard to gain freedom from pain due to unrealistic expectations. I was expecting my father to love me, and his actions show he was struggling with loving himself. Life has taught me that it is impossible to pour out of an empty cup.

My father's actions were valid proof that he was empty, and his emptiness spilled over to my mother and she started acting empty. It created a horrible domino effect that lasted for many years, even up to the birthing of this book. I could never quite figure out how to navigate through life without allowing pain to cripple me. There was just so much of it.

After my father pulled that little stunt by not allowing me to leave with him and my brothers, I couldn't wait for him to come back so I could get my stuff out of his car. Sunday at 6:00pm couldn't arrive fast enough. I made up my mind that I was done. He didn't have to worry about me anymore.

My dad pulled up and I stumped angrily to the car to grab my suitcase. I went in my room to unpack my clothes and the contents of my suitcase said find me. All my clothes were missing.

I ran to my brothers and asked them where my clothes were, and I said, "I bet the daughter of my father's wife took them." I cannot begin to express the rage I was feeling. First you treat me like an outsider and then you allow this stranger to take clothes you didn't pay for. I ran and told my mother. She jumped into mama mode, we jumped in the car, and drove to his house.

I didn't know what was about to happen, but I was prepared to fight. Enough is enough! When we arrived, I could see the girl standing in the window. This chick had the audacity to stand there and taunt me with my own clothes. My dad came outside with his delusional self and told my brothers to go in the house and look for the clothes.

There I was standing there livid because the girl is in the window with the clothes. My brothers come out empty handed. My mother starts yelling at my father and telling him the girl is in the window with the stuff. My father charges at my mother with the intent to harm her and I immediately jumped in front of her. I boldly said, "You may have beat her ass then, but you will NEVER touch her again!"

At that point, his wife came outside and started yelling for him to come in the house. This was a mess! I swear this man had a serious issue with me. You would take my clothes and give them to your stepdaughter. How cold and callous can you be? I had to push on from this. I don't know how I did it, but I managed to survive these massive blows to my soul.

My father wasn't the only hard thing I had to battle at during that time. Repeating the eighth grade was going to be difficult. My self-esteem was being annihilated based on the condition of my family and this wasn't going to help at all.

I remember the first day of school after moving back to Baytown. I was supposed to be getting on the ninth grade bus with my peers, but when the bus came, I just stood there. I had to wait for the eight grade bus. I wanted to run away and die. How could I face my peers? I didn't want to be classified as dumb or slow? I didn't need anyone else picking on me. I had enough of that going on from the man who was supposed to be protecting me from the bullies.

I felt like I was on an island all by myself. I started to really battle with my identity. I was having what they call an "identity crisis" because I didn't know who I was or where I fit. I didn't connect with certain people. I had friends but we didn't really click. They had advanced to having sex and doing drugs, but I wasn't into that. Then I was hanging with the eighth graders and they were immature, so I had to actually dummy myself down to get along and have some friends.

I can't tell you when I adapted to being in the eighth grade again, but I finally just got over the initial shock of it all. Then I started being teased for being heavy chested. This was another hurdle I had to cross. I couldn't hide my breast, like I couldn't hide the fact that I was in the eighth grade again. I had to learn to cope with it even though I didn't like it. My chest caused me to get unwanted attention from guys and jealousy from the girls. There was never a dull moment in my life. Something was always going on.

I started having some female issues and needed to see a doctor. My father was supposed to provide health insurance for me and my brothers according to the divorce decree, but my mother wasn't sure if he was complying. She reached out to my father about the insurance and the money to help pay for the visit. My mom told him what was going on and instead of being a concerned father he started yelling.

According to my mother, this man accused her of needing money for an abortion and said he wasn't giving her anything for me. My dad had done some pretty cruel stuff, but this was heart wrenching. He didn't even care about my health. As always, my mother figured out a way to get me to the doctor and they diagnosed me with having cyst on my ovaries.

Can you imagine going through something like this at such an early age? I hadn't even learned everything there was to know about that part of my body. Now I was battling emotionally and physically. Years later I learned how our spiritual state of being can affect the natural especially when you encounter consistent episodes of negativity. I was harboring so much negativity, dysfunction, and trauma at such an early age. I hadn't even really started to experience life, but it was already taking a toll on me.

During my years in high school, I simply just existed. I was a walking zombie. I spent so much time focusing on others and never really caring for myself. I was made to feel unimportant and invaluable to those who mattered most so I allowed everyone to treat me like this. I wanted to feel better. I was tired of carrying the pain and rehearsing it day after day. Wondering woulda, coulda, shoulda about my life and how different it could be. Nothing was changing so I started looking for coping methods.

One day I decided to drown my sorrows in a bottle of MD2020 and went to school drunk. I wasn't thinking about the negative affect this would have on my life. I mean do we ever consider the impact that negative reactions have on our lives? No, we just jump off the cliff hoping to land in a better place. Drinking was only going to land me in a place filled with more trauma, but I couldn't see that then.

I was tired!

My mother won the house in the divorce, but that didn't keep us from being poor. The only problem was I didn't know we were poor. My mother always taught us that everyone was equal, but one day I found out that wasn't true.

I let some friends come over to the house without permission. One of them looked in the refrigerator and saw we didn't have any food. This was so embarrassing! We were all standing around when I heard my mother pull up. She came home earlier than I anticipated. I told everyone to run out the back door. In a panic I forgot that the door wasn't connected to the door hinges.

Everyone else was already out the house, but when I ran through the door it fell on me and they all stopped and started laughing. Could my life get any worse? Here I was trying to fit in and still managed to humiliate myself. The title of this chapter is, "Why Me, Lord?" because it appeared that I was a moving target for adversity. No matter where I went, what I did, or who I did it with something crazy was bound to happen in my life.

Chapter Four
"Looking For A Substitute"

The word "substitute" is defined according to Webster as a person or thing acting or serving in place of another. It is sad to say, but this is where I found myself. I started looking for other males to act or serve in the place of my father. There was a deep hole that I assumed could be filled by someone other than the man who caused it.

I started dating this guy and he was not attractive AT ALL! Just thinking about it makes me want to go back in time and slap my teenage self. Lord knows I wasn't attracted to him and to make matters worse I allowed him to take my virginity.

Talk about desperately seeking for love. I was truly seeking in all the wrong places. I was so empty I didn't care how I got filled. It was like being thirsty and the only thing available to quench my thirst was toilet water. Sorry, but it was that bad!

My first sexual encounter was horrible because I was under the assumption that something magical was supposed to happen. This is why you shouldn't listen to other people and be easily influenced by their actions. What works for others, might not work for you. Eventually, we broke up and I met this guy from Houston. He was a really nice guy and wasn't bad looking either. He would buy me nice things, but for some reason I wasn't feeling him.

Now that I'm older I realize that I wanted a bad guy. I didn't want the guy who was nice, sweet, and kind because I had experienced nothing but abuse and rejection to this point. I didn't know what nice and normal looked like. Then I met this other guy who was a total bomb and I was head over heels for him. The classic case of rejection, dysfunction, and low self-esteem intertwined together.

One day we were sitting at the park and this car pulled up and blocked us in. The two guys in the car just sat there. We had no idea what was going on. I was nervous but we couldn't drive off. If they would have opened fire on us, we would have both been dead. The car started backing up and pulled away. I guess something was supposed to happen, but they changed their mind or God was doing something for us that we couldn't do for ourselves.

After that we hung out but not as much. He called me one day and said he was moving out of town and wanted me to go with him. I thought about it, but we didn't have a job or money. I told him that it was nice knowing him, but he could go without me. That was the last time I ever spoke to him.

I met this new guy who was another nice one that took me to see Big Daddy Kane in concert. He would open doors for me and treat me like a young lady. I literally called him and said I didn't want to see him anymore. No, he didn't do anything wrong. I didn't feel like I deserved to be treated with dignity and respect based on the warped relationship with my father.

There are so many women who have been in this same place and everyone responds differently. I have had people tell me to get over it, but parental abandonment and rejection doesn't just go away. You must be intentional about dealing with the pain because it will definitely deal with you.

I was struggling to develop a healthy relationship with myself, so God knows having a healthy relationship with a man was out of the question. I was so confused during this phase of my life. I wanted a substitute, but this wasn't working in my favor.

I couldn't look to my mother because in my opinion we were pretty much in the same boat, looking to fill the void that this man left behind. We were both suffering and battling with an identity crisis. My mother was still trying to find herself after the pain, abuse, and abandonment. The only difference was she could find another man, but I couldn't find another father.

Even if she married another man, he could never replace the man whose blood was running warm in my veins. The man God chose to be the steward, teacher, and protector over my life. I could never get back the time lost between us. I remember being in the tenth grade and I was having such a hard time with this daddy stuff.

My school counselor called me in the office and told me to write down everything I felt about him. I was somewhat apprehensive at first, but I did as she instructed. Her plan was to give my father the letter. As an adult I asked him if he ever received the letter and he said no. I guess it didn't really matter, but I can say that her suggestion helped a little bit. I was able to release a lot of the anger page by page. Yet, life for me had to go on whether I wanted it to or not. I was determined to find the perfect substitute.

My mother and I went to the store one day. I was walking up and down the aisles when I spotted this very handsome young man. I was not about to miss the opportunity to get his number, so I walked up to him and boldly asked for it. Yeah, I know the boy usually does the asking, but I wasn't taking any chances.

My mother saw us talking and hinted that he was "the one" and that she could tell he was genuinely nice. He had his own car and was working to assist his dad with the bills because he lost his job. As fine as he was the "good guy" siren started going off in my head. He was just too good to be true.

He lost his mother and it was obvious that he had great respect for his father. He was the ideal guy for any young woman looking to fall in love and have a bright future. My mother kept emphasizing that he was "the one" and I wasn't trying to hear it. We went on our first date and he was such a gentleman. He was doing all the right things, but I was still apprehensive.

While we were dating his birthday came around and my mother made me get him a German chocolate cake and some balloons. When I presented the cake and balloons to him, he was so excited. I know you are going to think I'm crazy, but I didn't like him or so I thought. All this took place in 1990 during my senior year. He even took me to my senior prom. He was the guy you would be proud to bring home to meet your parents. He just wasn't the guy for me. He was the perfect gentlemen, but eventually I cut off the relationship.

I was just that emotionally and mentally damaged. He was "the one" I let slip through my fingers as the old folks would say. I believe we could have built something together. I was graduating from school and ready to embark on a new adventure, but I was afraid of love. I was afraid to try something different because I didn't know what different looked like.

My life was consumed with toxic relationships, therefore, anything nontoxic didn't sit well with me. It felt like it was too good to be true and that overtime it would end up like what I faced my whole life.

I regret not allowing myself to open up and experience love and life. I was locked in a cage that I couldn't escape from, no matter how hard I tried. I thought a substitute would work. The substitute wasn't the problem. All along the problem was me!!!!

Chapter Five
"No Longer A Child"

The bible says, "When I was a child, I thought like a child; but when I became an adult, I put away childish things." This is an incredibly unique scripture that people quote all the time, but I have learned throughout life that there are a lot of adults who still think and act like children (this is just a side note).

I can't honestly say if I was excited about becoming an adult because I had experienced so much as a child. I needed a mental break from life, but in my mother's eyes she was ready for me to get to work. She was so ready that she took it upon herself to go to Walmart and tell the people in the snack bar that I needed a job. She came home excited to tell me about an interview for a job I didn't apply for.

I went on the interview and was hired on the spot. My mom was taking me back and forth to work every day. One day she blurted out, "I'm tired so you are going to drive. Stay within the lines and stop at red and go on green." I had never been in the driver's seat a day in my life. That day I learned how to drive and have been driving ever since.

I was talking to this guy and one day he asked me why I didn't have a car. To be honest I had never thought about it. Beyond my better judgement I decided to reach out to my dad and ask if he could get me a car. He hadn't really done anything else and he bought my stepsister a car so why not ask.

This man said, "Pick out the car, get the insurance and the down payment, and I will meet you at the dealership." I replied, "If I have to do all that then what do I need you for!" I hung up the phone in his face.

From that point forward I made up my mind that I would go the extra mile to provide for me. Walmart employees were given the option to purchase stock in the company. I purchased some stock and that is how I bought my first car. It was a silver Ford Tempo with grey interior. Don't tell me what God won't do when you make up your mind to work hard and press past the drama and foolishness in life.

I could have easily got in my feelings and allowed his rejection to stop me. He actually helped me by saying no because it sparked a flame within my soul that caused me to go after life and to finally take control of my emotions, verses letting them control me.

When the big twenty-one came I was super excited and ready to hit the clubs. There was a club in Southwest Houston called Jamaica-Jamaica and that was the destination for my first birthday party. Yes, in twenty-one years, I had never been given a birthday party. My cake and balloons were really nice. I was on top of the world. You couldn't tell me nothing that night.

I met this guy named Fred during the party who could really dance. He was the life of the party. I had so much fun I started clubbing all the time. From the age of twenty-one to thirty-one I was wilding out and going to the club every day of the week except Friday.

When I turned twenty-two, I was hanging out with a girl who worked with me at Walmart. We decided to go to a hole in the wall in Brennett, Texas. The music was nice, and the ambiance was mellow. I sat there sipping on my drink and minding my business since I was the new girl in the club. I looked up and my eyes landed on this guy whose smile mesmerized me.

He was tall, dark, and handsome. I guess he knew I was checking him out because he came over and introduced himself as Craig. I wanted to fall out the chair, but I had to play it cool.

He asked me to dance. So, I stood up and followed him to the dance floor. We were having such a great time. We danced to a couple of songs and then sat down at the bar to get acquainted. He started telling me about his kids and that he had some gifts in the back of his truck he needed to drop off to them. He asked if I wanted to ride with him.

He was fine, but I wasn't about to leave with a total stranger. I declined the offer and he didn't press the issue. He simply asked for my number and left. I wasn't sure if I would ever see or hear from him again. I was dating a guy name Jason, but he wasn't all that. Two days later Craig called, and I was so excited. He asked me out on a date, and I accepted. Craig agreed to pick me up, but there was one problem, Jason was at my house.

When Craig knocked on the door, I didn't panic not one bit. I opened the door and told Jason that he could stay, but I was going on a date. The irony of it all was that Jason and Craig knew each other. It should have been awkward, but I didn't care at this point. My eyes were on the prize and I wasn't about to let anyone, or anything stop me from getting it.

I walked out and closed the door. When we got in the truck Craig said he couldn't believe that I did Jason like that. Oh well it is what it is! I reached the point where a man couldn't tell me nothing. I thought I was the best thing since sliced bread. I didn't care about a man or his feelings. I was doing me, and you could either fall in line or get dismissed and make room for the next one.

My daddy taught me that anyone is replaceable. In the streets, they say, "What one won't do, the next one will!" Thank God I'm saved today because I was a force to be reckoned with.

On another note, while he was worrying about Jason, I felt a slight draft near my feet in the truck. I wasn't sure what was going on, so I looked down and to my surprise I was able to see the road while we were driving. The man had a hole in the floor of his truck. This should have been a HUGE sign to run, but I was caught up in the looks and never thought to concern myself with what he had or didn't have.

I will not lie it didn't take no time for me to fall head over heels in love with this man. At some point we decided to take the relationship further.

I went to his house one day to spend the night. Keep in mind that he had kids with another woman. I wasn't sure what his life consisted of outside of me, but it became very apparent that he had some drama going on. When we got up the next morning his two front tires were on flat and the two tires on the driver's side of my car facing the street were on flat. I didn't know what to say, but the situation got worse when my mother showed up.

I was still living with my mother at the time and I failed to inform her that I wasn't coming home, even though I was grown. As a concerned mother she went on a quest to find me and when she did, I was so embarrassed. She looked at me and then looked at my car and shook her head. Craig said he would take care of the tires, but that didn't sit well with my mother.

She looked at me with disappointment and said something I should have taken to heart and truly read between the lines, but I didn't get it. She said, "He is the type of man who will buy you two used tires!" I didn't understand why it mattered as long as he fixed the tires. My mother had lived much longer than me and could spot a trifling man from a mile away. Quite naturally I thought she was overreacting.

As much as I hate to admit this, my mother was right. He went and bought two used tires. When I pulled up in the driveway it felt like my mother was waiting to prove me wrong. She saw the used tires and went off. She said, "Now your dumb ass is going to give me the money to buy two new tires because you are used to new, not used!" I couldn't say a word.

After many years of being in the relationship I became a professional of all things used and raggedy. The quote, "You become what you surround yourself with" is so true.

My mom peeped game, but my nose was so wide open that I couldn't see anything but him. I didn't care about what he had or didn't have. I didn't care about the children and the crazy baby mama. I just wanted him. I cant even tell you what I liked about him other than his looks. I feel like he was sent on assignment to make my life a living hell. I was living in a mirage because he was showing me one thing but doing something different.

We dated for quite some time, but it started to feel like the relationship wasn't moving forward. One day we were in the car going somewhere and I decided to ask him where the relationship was going. I opened my big mouth and used the "M" word. I said, "I would love to get married." He replied with, "I never thought about it, that would be a good idea." This is how he proposed, and we became engaged.

We got married in 1994. My mother decorated the church and his family did the reception. I always wanted to be a wife and a mother. I just didn't realize at the time that I was trying to force it to happen. The bible says, "When a man finds a wife, he finds a good thing!" Well I can't say he found me because I was the one who bought it up and simply agreed.

Maybe I desperately wanted what I never had. A loving family with a devoted husband and father, with children I could love, nurture, and provide a solid family foundation. Whatever the reason, I can honestly say this was the worse decision I ever made in my life.

I had NO idea what I signed up for and who I chose to become one with.

I was no longer a child, but I wish my mother would have hit me upside my head and knocked some sense into me. She tried to warn me, but I didn't listen. The seasoned saints used to say, "A hard head, makes a soft behind" and believe me, my behind was definitely soft after all the bumps and humps on the road to misery.

Chapter Six
"Signs Ignored"

I f it looks like a duck and quacks like a duck, don't try to make it a chicken. There are so many people in life who refuse to see the glass half full. We want the glass to be overflowing, and though I hate to burst your bubble, there are times when the glass is completely empty. I tried so many times to fill Craig's glass, because it was bone dry, it wasn't even half full. But if I be honest my glass wasn't full either. I was trying to pour from an empty place, which is why I felt I needed him.

In some distorted way I thought he could make me better, happy, and more fulfilled. Man was I wrong! As the marriage progressed, he only made me bitter, unhappy, and extremely unfulfilled. There were so many signs, but I ignored them all. Don Draper said, "People will show you who they are, but we ignore it because we want them to be who we want them to be."

I had to learn this the hard way. I was trying to make Craig save me from drowning, while he was sinking in quicksand.

Marriage was a major step and God knows I hadn't thought this all the way through. It sounded good, but this was a life changing decision. Well, you know how we do, the still small voice was screaming no, but the people pleaser in me was saying I don't want to let him down. It wasn't long before the signs started manifesting. The first sign I ignored was the Thursday before the wedding. I asked someone where Craig was, and they said he was at his sister's friend house.

I went to pick him up and he came out the house fully dressed, but home chick came out in a robe. Now, I didn't have any reason to believe that my soon to be husband would cheat on me just days before our wedding. I was wrong again! I didn't have proof then, but I later found out they had been sleeping together before we met and while we were dating. He was a cold piece of work, but I was in to deep and couldn't break away.

The second sign telling me to run came with the bridesmaid dresses. I got into a disagreement with the seamstress who refused to finish the dresses. I had to pay her for unfinished work just to get the dresses and take them somewhere else to be completed. I was overwhelmed and extremely frustrated. I went to my girlfriend's house and I said, "If my mother hadn't spent money putting this wedding together, I wouldn't be getting married." By this time, I felt obligated because she had invested so much of her own money. I wish I would have opened my mouth and told the truth.

Then to make matters worse. I wanted my father to give me away. Don't ask me why, I guess that is every daughter dream whether the father has been there or not. I called him expecting some enthusiasm and support being I was his oldest daughter. As always, he had something fly to say. He agreed to give me away if I purchased the tux for him and my brother. I asked this man for something simple and he still couldn't do it without condition. After breaking down to Craig, he went and confronted my dad and he told Craig he was just joking.

The day of the wedding came, and I was so tensed up and nervous. I knew there was no going back after this, but my pride wouldn't let me walk away. Even though I felt like I was walking into a battlefield I was too afraid to hurt him. The classic tale of a rejected woman. Always too afraid to hurt the other person at the expense of hurting yourself. I made up my mind to smile and go through the motions.

My father actually showed up to walk me down the aisle. The wedding coordinator was prolonging the process for some reason and it was about to pour down raining. We finally decided to start the wedding. It was your typical wedding ceremony. We looked the part, but I can't really say how I felt. The hard part was over, and it was time for the reception. We hadn't been married an hour before the chronicles of Craig broke out. The reception took place at a convention center in Brennett, Texas not far from the church.

Craig and I walk in as the newly married couple and begin mingling with the guests. This random woman walks up to me and says she is a friend of Craig and ask to see my wedding ring. This was rather odd because she didn't appear to be too excited about the nuptials. My women's intuition picked up on her scorned female vibes. It was as if he proposed to her once before and she wanted to make sure it wasn't the same ring. I later found out he was sleeping with her too.

The time came for us to leave our guests behind and head off to enjoy our honeymoon. What should have been a relaxing time to love on each other, turned to us hating on each other. After arguing he suggested we leave and go back to the apartment, but he didn't have the keys because he borrowed his uncles' car for us to drive something decent on our wedding day. We finally found a cheap motel to stay in for the night. There are no words to describe how sad I was. My emotions were through the roof.

More than anything, I was disappointed in myself for not choosing me. He was slowly showing me that he was worthless and lacked character and integrity, but I didn't have the courage to speak up. I had no clue what that looked like. I had become accustomed to going along to get along and this was another one of those times. I was in my early twenties and after all that time I still hadn't learned how to value myself. I was looking for validation in someone else. I thought I could fix him, but I needed fixing.

The first year of marriage was a living hell. Craig was working, but when we got married, I lost my job. We struggled trying to live off one salary. I could feel a piece of me break every day. I tried doing so many things to make him happy. I wanted him to notice me and acknowledge me as his wife, but nothing worked. Since I wasn't working, I would go to his mother's house to keep her company. I thought he would appreciate his wife taking interest in his mother. This man had the nerve to yell at me to stay home because I was using too much gas. Too much gas! Like it was my fault that we were broke and didn't have much money.

He told me that I needed to figure something out in regard to our financial hardships. I was absolutely lost because he was the head of the household not me. He wanted to beat his chest and say he was the man, without acting like a man. A real man wouldn't let his family struggle. I was married to him, plus he still had kids to take care of as well. God knows I was trying extremely hard, but he wasn't making it easy at all.

I even tried to learn how to cook and that wasn't enough to satisfy him. I would try to be supportive when he did work by at least asking how his day was. He would look at me and tell me not to ask about his damn day. This man had me on an emotional roller coaster. I was all over the place. I couldn't help but wonder why this man agreed to marry me if he was going to treat me like an outsider. We could have continued to hang out and be friends until I got tired or until the real Craig showed up.

By the grace of God, we made it to one full year in the marriage. I wanted to do something for our anniversary, and he said we couldn't because we had the kids that week. I messed around and asked if the kids could stay with their mom. What did I say that for? He responded with a very nasty attitude and said, "I don't give a damn about no anniversary!" Needless to say, we spent the anniversary with his kids.

I was torn on the inside! I didn't have much fight left! It felt like I was being tolerated and he was the one who was inadequate, but he made me feel so low. If I had any confidence, he was stripping it away. All I knew was that I didn't want to fail. I didn't want to repeat the life I lived with my parents. I guess that was my mistake. There life was theirs and I couldn't control what happened to them, but I couldn't see that.

I wanted to be married and even though times were hard I was committed to making it work. I didn't get married to turn around and get divorced. When it came to intimacy in the relationship, I became the pursuer. He didn't come on to me at all. Before we got married, he was all over me, but now it was different. He had me questioning myself in so many areas. Was I not attractive enough anymore? Did I not turn him on?

I knew he had to be cheating so when I confronted him, he actually told me yes, like I was supposed to give him some brownie points for being honest. Then to top it all off he would try to justify his infidelity by saying he had an understanding with the women because they knew he wasn't leaving me for them. I can't begin to say how many times I wanted to do harm to that man, but I kept hoping and praying it would get better. He would tell me how much he loved me but follow it up with "I just get caught up sometimes!"

I just get caught up sometimes!!!! I had to repeat that for the sake of wondering how I even accepted such a lame excuse, but unfortunately, I did. When I ponder over this particular time in my life, I just shake my head and thank God that He allowed me to make it out of this whirlwind I landed myself in.

Chapter Seven
"Blinded By Insecurities"

B eing insecure is dangerous to ones mental, physical, emotional, financial, and spiritual health. If left undetected and unhealed being insecure can ruin individuals, marriages, businesses, churches, and the list goes on. Many times, people don't even know they are battling with insecurities because we know how to make ourselves look good. We learn at an early age how to walk the walk and talk the talk.

We learn how to make ourselves appear to be more than we are simply because we want to fit in and be accepted. This is a dangerous dysfunction that was ruling every aspect of my life. Not only was I insecure, but Craig was insecure as well. It didn't seem that way because I was basing it on looks but looks without any substance or integrity is a disaster waiting to happen.

I can't believe I fooled myself into believing that he could be my saving grace. I just knew he was the one to make all my man hurt from my father and previous men dissolve, but if I tell the truth I married my father. This man, much like my father had it out for me and at first, I didn't know why. Today, I understand that he needed help just as much as I did. Any man who refuses to be committed to his wife is battling with some deep rooted issues. It was like he was trying to prove he was a man through intimacy because he was suffering in the areas that mattered most like working, character, integrity, and trust.

It doesn't take a rocket scientist to have sex, but it takes integrity, dedication, and drive to be man enough to get out of self to provide for your family. He just didn't have what it takes, and I missed those important characteristics during our courtship. I was mesmerized by the flesh, but never once considered the condition of his heart or his spirit. This man had the gift of gab. His conversation ruled the nation and I fell for every word.

When he opened his mouth to speak, it was like he was casting a spell on me. No matter how crazy it was I fell for the banana in the tailpipe every time. This man refused to remain faithful. He bounced back and forth between me and his ex-women every time he got the urge to run back to them. It was rather weird because he just appeared to have it together. He didn't mess with nobody. He wasn't confrontational. He looked like the ideal gentlemen, but he was a wolf in sheep's clothing.

Many would say he was being a typical man, but I disagree. If you want to be a typical man, do that without including a wife because that was unfair to me. If he would have been upfront from the jump and said Yulanda I am really not the committed type, I have several women friends; I could have taken that much better than being his wife and constantly being cheated on.

I was already insecure before I entered the relationship. I was treading on thin ice, but he broke the ice and I started to drown in the freezing water. I found myself becoming cold and bitter. He was taking my kindness for weakness. He was using the fact that all these women wanted him to break me down and the crazy thing is, sometimes I found myself wanting him more. The bible is truly clear when it says the heart is deceitfully wicked and no one can understand it.

It wasn't making any sense. I watched my mama go through this and swore up and down that I would never be her and here I was walking in her same footsteps. It was ridiculous because the women he would cheat with didn't even compare to me. Now, let me be clear I would never put another woman down, but I'm simply saying he had eighty at home, but preferred to cheat with a twenty. There was nothing I wouldn't do to make him happy.

Which now I know that was the problem. I should have been focusing on my own happiness, but I didn't know what that looked like. Craig made me laugh, which means we should have stayed in the friend zone. We should have never crossed the line to enter into a committed relationship that required sacrifice and selflessness.

When it all boils down, we were two broken individuals who were feeding off each other's brokenness. He was using me, and I was using him. We were using each other and, in the end, neither one of us won. To the outside world we looked happy. We put those mask on, well let me rephrase, I put my mask on and made it work. He was going to be him no matter what. I was the one hiding the truth behind a fake smile and the invisible tears I cried in my heart day in and day out.

You would think he understood my struggles because he didn't have a relationship with his father either. We had so much in common, but our responses to love, life, relationships, and responsibilities were absolutely different. The whole relationship was a joke, but I learned many valuable lessons. I learned a lot about myself. I learned a lot about men and women. I guess since I wasn't gaining anything else, I might as well gain some wisdom and revelation in the process.

It wasn't long before I learned some other interesting facts about by dear ex-husband. When we got married Craig told me that he had two children. These children were by the woman who cut my tires when we first started dating. Let me not leave out that he was still sleeping with her while he was dating me, which is why she cut my tires. I guess that was her ghetto way of letting me know I was treading on her territory.

Well, turns out he had another daughter whom I met that was twelve years old. I found out about this daughter because the mother kicked her out. Yes, I couldn't believe it either. How do you kick out a twelve year old? Well, I guess I can relate since my father didn't want me in his house. The daughter called the house looking for her father, but I answered the phone because Craig was out of town. She asked if she could come and live with us.

I reached out to Craig and he basically said it was up to me. I wasn't about to let a twelve year old be out on the street, so I said yes. I didn't even have time to process the fact that he didn't tell me about this other child. We dated and had been married for quite some time and not even one word. This man was something else, but there is more.

In 2001, I was minding my own business when I was confronted by a friend who asked me had we moved into a new apartment. I told him no and asked why. He said he had been seeing Craig's truck in the complex. Well this was weird because I didn't know anyone who lived there. I went home and I asked Craig who lived in the apartments. He had this guilty look on his face, followed by, "I need to talk to you." This meant some bull was getting ready to come out of his mouth, but believe me, nothing could have prepared me for what he was about to say.

I expected him to say what he always said and that was him sleeping with another woman. He admitted to sleeping with another woman, but the circumstances surrounding the woman almost took me out. He said and I quote, "I have been going over there because I got this girl pregnant and I was checking on her. Matter of fact, she is getting ready to have the baby anytime today and I need to go to the hospital because she is on crack and they are going to take the baby if no one is there."

I was speechless! I was boiling on the inside. It wasn't bad enough that he was still cheating, but to cheat with a woman on crack, get her pregnant, and now you need to ride off into the sunset to save her and your unborn child. This man was stretching me beyond my limit. What type of person in their right mind does this to another human being? This was beyond low! He really hit below the belt with this one.

After I picked my face up off the ground, I built up the courage to speak and I said, "If you leave this house, don't come back!" He said, "But my son is being born!" I told him he had to choose between me and his son. He contemplated his next move and he must have known I was serious because he didn't leave. I don't know why, but I felt sorry him because he broke down and started crying about not being able to see his son. At that time, I didn't care, I felt I had to take a stand for me.

He failed to consider my feelings, so why should I consider his. A couple days later we found out the mother delivered the baby and was taken to jail for having crack cocaine in her system while being pregnant. The woman's grandmother was at the hospital and took custody of the baby while the mother was incarcerated. I felt so sorry for this innocent baby who didn't ask to be born into this mess.

I finally went by myself to see the baby. The lady came to the door holding the baby and there was no doubt that he was Craig' son. She looked at me and said I was a beautiful woman. I said thank you and expressed how sorry I felt for the child and the situation he was in. I left and never saw the baby again until years later.

I must admit I didn't see this coming. I mean when I think about it, this man didn't have enough integrity to protect himself from getting another woman pregnant or bringing me an STD. The fact that she was on crack speaks volumes to the lifestyle she was living and there is no telling how many people she had been with prior to him. This was crazy, but this had become my life.

I hate to say this, but I'm not sure which one is worse, getting physically beat by a man or mentally and emotionally beat by a man. I've heard physical scars will heal, but these scars he was causing were digging deeper and deeper into my soul. These were the types of scars that went unseen by others. I didn't have to cover them up because they were internal. My mind was all over the place. I wanted to run away, but I didn't know how.

Six years of marriage and we still had no children of our own. Can you imagine how I felt as a woman knowing that another woman produced a baby for my husband? He was so adamant about protecting her and needing to go to his child and that really did something to me. I wondered if he would be the same towards me or would he continue being cold and callous.

Since he was making babies, it was evident that he wasn't having any issues reproducing. I still hadn't conceived, and it started to worry me because I wanted children of my own. I was helping him to raise his children, but it's nothing like having that experience for yourself. I decided to undergo a procedure that would determine if there was something going on with my reproductive system.

This was a process I had to endure by myself because Craig could never understand what I was going through. To be honest I don't even think he cared. He was doing him and didn't have a problem flaunting it in my face. I found myself praying and asking God why I had to care for another woman's children and not have my own.

I never received the answer to that question. I continued to play with the hand God dealt to me. He is the one who gives life and overtime I found peace in loving the children I was raising. I did my best to give them what I never had; despite the challenges I was experiencing with their father.

Chapter Eight
"He Just Won't Quit"

The definition of "insanity" is doing the same thing over and over again, yet expecting a different result. Let me be the first to admit I was mentally and emotionally insane. I allowed this man to manipulate me for years in the name of what ... love! This wasn't love because love doesn't hurt like this. I was dealing with a false sense of responsibility.

I convinced myself that I was responsible for his feelings and emotions, but he didn't have to be responsible for mine. I didn't want to hurt him by leaving, but he was hurting me by staying. I couldn't trust this man for nothing in the world. I don't even know how he slept at night without being convicted. He would definitely give Denzel Washington a run for his money. He deserved an Oscar for some of the things he pulled off.

One summer he planned a trip to Disney for him and the kids. I just so happened to be talking to the oldest daughter one day after we divorced, and she brought up the trip and confessed that they stopped off in Georgia to get her little brother. Craig never admitted it, but this was a baby everyone knew about except me. Here I was taking care of his daughter all them years and she never said anything. This son was "only a year older than the son he had with the woman on crack. So, this was another baby born during the marriage.

Oh, the story gets better! The mother of Craig's oldest daughter got pregnant and had another baby while she was living with us. One day she asked if her little sister could come over. Well, I didn't have a problem with it because it was her sister and I'm sure she wanted to spend time with her. The baby came to visit. While we were sitting around the baby would follow Craig and yell out "daddy" over and over again.

I approached Craig and said, "You need to stop her from calling you daddy, before she gets confused." He laughed it off and kept doing what he was doing. Well turns out the baby was calling him daddy because it was his child. Again, the joke was on me. He had been sleeping with his daughters' mother and got her pregnant, but since she was also married the baby was passed off as her husbands' child. Again, he didn't confess the truth until years later.

This man was betraying me left and right, but I still couldn't pack my bags to leave. I'm sure when I didn't leave after the first child, he pretty much figured I would take anything. This was past insanity. I was breathing, but I wasn't living. I don't even think I was existing. This man had no respect for me whatsoever. The women he was sleeping with would smile in my face and act like we were good knowing they were being fraud. I was mad at them, but I couldn't blame them because Craig opened these doors and allowed these soul ties to fester and infect our marriage.

His daughters were having a military ball. I went shopping and bought me a dress for the ball and the girls saw it. On the night of the ball his oldest daughter's mother whom he impregnated showed up in the same exact dress. I was livid! I felt so betrayed by the girls, and the mother. I ran to the restroom and she ran in another direction, but my husband ran after her and not after me. Then to make matters worse his other baby mama was there laughing during the whole incident.

While in the restroom I called my friend and after venting she convinced me to join the ball and make the best of it. I had finally reached the point of no return. I was tired of making the best of things. I vowed that I would stay until the girls graduated high school. They didn't have long to go so to make sure I didn't change my mind, I started packing without him noticing. To make matters worse he ended up losing his job as a truck driver. I was working, but I wasn't about to foot the bills by myself, so I told him I couldn't afford the bills.

I suggested asking his daughters to pitch in because they were both working, but he objected to that idea. Since he didn't want to work, bad got worse. When the water and lights got cut off, we had to go to his mother's house to take baths. This was past embarrassing. After eleven years of marriage it had come to this. This man had made a complete mockery of me the entire marriage and now he wouldn't even force himself to provide for me.

I forced myself to remain in this hell thinking I was doing it for him, and I couldn't even cut on the light switch or bathe after a long day's work. How much more inconvenience was I supposed to take? I know I should have been gone, but I didn't leave. I couldn't go back and change what already happened. I had to make up my mind to do something new that didn't include him.

I had given him enough of my time. After some months, he took a job out of town and it worked in my favor. While he was gone, I started taking my stuff out the house bit by bit. I called my mother to say I needed a place to stay but she didn't believe me because I had left before and went right back. So, she said no. I was angry at first, but then I had to respect it once I cooled down. I can only imagine what she felt and was thinking as she watched the years of my life play out, especially after warning me of the kind of man he was. I dealt with his torture for years. I decided to call my aunt and she said I could come and stay with her.

One day he came home early, and he was in the bedroom. He could see that some things around the house were missing, so he said, "Is there something we need to talk about?" I replied, "Yes, I am leaving! You have disrespected me a long time, but enough is enough!" He said, "But we have bills to pay and I just started working!" Just like a selfish person. He didn't say anything about me, only what he needed. Then he asked me if I was sure if I was going to leave. He said, "Well since you are leaving, I have something I need to tell you. The baby girl and oldest son of my oldest daughters' mother are both mine!"

Since I was leaving, I guess he felt the need to confess his lies. He never verbally confessed to the last two children being his during the marriage. I stood there in shock and said, "I should have known!" I went on to say, "What's good for you is that I packed my gun away from this house because I would kill you!"

At this moment, the insanity truly kicked in because I wanted to kill him. I was willing to risk going to prison which at that time wouldn't have mattered because I had been in prison anyway. The only difference is I wasn't locked up behind bars. I thank God for this all the time. He would not have been worth me giving up the remaining years of my life for.

I walked away from him and called his daughter's mother. When she answered I said, "You are low down and dirty. I took care of your child, gave you my clothes and you still had sex with my husband and made a child!" There was nothing she could say or that I wanted to hear so I hung up in her face. At that point I was like a turkey on Christmas...done! I left and quite naturally he came looking for me. He didn't know where I was going so, he went by my brother's house. I mean why act like you care now.

He wasn't searching for me during the marriage. Then if you really pay attention, he was used to revolving doors. He kept all his past women in rotation, and I guess he thought I would do the same. Nope! I turned in my resignation from Team Craig. From the looks of it he had enough players. Even though I was benched most of the times I still showed up and tried to be a team player. It was time for me to go back to the drawing board and get my life in order.

Once I disconnected myself all the deep dark dirty secrets started to come out. His family knew about all seven of his children and never broke the code. This man had not one, not two, but THREE children during our eleven years of marriage. I tried to come up with several reasons why I endured such heartache. I even went as far as thinking I was being punished for my actions during high school when I would act cold and callous towards people.

The bible does tell us that we reap what we sow, but I hadn't done anyone that bad to deserve all this man put me through. The crazy thing is after I left, I still felt sorry for him. We would talk here and there, but to be honest his life went to hell once I was gone. The grace he had upon his life due to me being his wife was gone and over. Speaking of grace, let me testify that God's grace was truly with me.

There is no telling how many women this man actually slept with during the marriage. The fact that God never allowed him to bring me a sexually transmitted disease shows that God was truly with me. He could have contracted a disease that was incurable and killed us both. God was doing for me what I couldn't do for myself. I didn't have enough sense to protect me. The seasoned saints used to say, "God takes care of babies and fools!"

Well, today I am not ashamed to say that I was being a fool. Was it a fool for love? No, that went out the window. I was simply being a fool from fear. I was afraid of being alone and unsure of what life would be without him. He finally forced my hand and fear or not I realized I didn't want to be a fool anymore.

It was time to put my big girl undies on and be the woman I was destined to be. God was getting ready to introduce me to the purpose He created within me before I entered my mother's womb and was introduced to this cruel world. Craig and I officially divorced in 2005.

Chapter Nine
"Bridging The Gap"

A "gap" is defined as an unfilled space or interval, a break in continuity. As I travel back over the roads I've traveled, I have experienced many gaps in my life. There was a gap from my parent's divorce. There was a gap from my father's rejection. There was a gap from my mother's abandonment. There was a gap from repeating the eighth grade. There were several gaps during the marriage, therefore it is safe to say that my life has been filled with a plethora of gaping holes.

I spent so many years of my life feeling empty and alone. I battled with not being good enough and not belonging or fitting in. I know what it feels like to be in a crowded room but still feel invisible. I also know what it feels like to be in a crowded room and the looks and stares are of sheer disgust. I have spent countless years trying to figure out why my journey had to be so hard.

I knew about God, but I sometimes wondered if He had a personal vendetta against me because I couldn't get genuine love from no one. There were times that I questioned my existence and wondered why I was born to suffer at the hands of those who were supposed to nurture and train me. None of my life was making sense. It appeared that no matter where I went or who I connected to there was a problem. It appeared that I was the problem and for many years I lived my life in offence because of it.

Offense is a dangerous stronghold that has the power to destroy your life. My life was being controlled and consumed by offense, but God didn't reveal it to me until I got to the end of writing this book. I was so busy living my life trying to bury the past and act like it didn't happen that it was still controlling and consuming me. Out of sight, out of mind is not a true statement. You might not be thinking about things of the past, but that doesn't mean you are not carrying it in your heart or that your soul is not still wounded.

The easiest way to know if you are battling offense, is when every little thing sets you off. People could say the sun is red and you find some way to get offended or make the red sun about you. Living with offense leads to a life filled with negativity which results in a miserable life. It is extremely hard to be around or in a relationship with an offended person. He or she never sees themselves, it is always someone else. Well, let me say this, there is a root to offense and for many it starts at childhood.

When you are constantly bullied, mistreated, unloved, unnoticed, rejected, or tossed around you learn ways to defend yourself. This means you are constantly fighting for position and trying to prove that you are qualified or worthy. You develop the I'm going to get them before they get me mentality. This is a hard way to live and it does damage to the physical body. Negativity takes a lot of energy we could be using for something helpful and positive.

I'm sure I have missed out on some good things in life because I was broken, wounded, and offended. I may have forfeited some blessings because I didn't know how to properly respond to a situation or circumstance. I was under the impression that not dealing with certain people or cutting off toxic relationships was enough, but its not. There has to be an intentional time of healing and deliverance that must manifest. Healing isn't automatic.

When you get sick with a cold, that is a sign that infection has settled someone in your body. If you don't be intentional about seeing the doctor, taking medication, increasing your vitamin C, and resting, the cold will remain and over time get worse. Well pain, hurt, disappointment, and offense are mental and emotional infections that can alter the course of your life if not healed. I know people who have been living a defeated life for years with no way of escape. This is not Gods will for our lives.

There is a powerful quote by an unknown author that says, "An unhealed person can find offense in pretty much anything someone does. A healed person understands that the actions of others has absolutely nothing to do with them. Each day you get to decide which one you will be."

I can remember the day that this quote manifested in my life. My marriage to Craig had been over for about three years and within this time frame I lost my best friend who I was extremely close with. This took me into a low place where I felt disconnected from life itself. I wasn't diagnosed as having depression, but that is how distorted I felt.

I was going to a church in Brennett, Texas but to be honest it was only for the sake of saying I went. My body was present, but my mind, will, soul, spirit, and emotions were absent. I needed something different.

In Mark 4 it talks about Jesus teaching and healing the people, but in Mark 4:35 it says, "When that evening came, He said to His disciples, "Let us cross to the other side." Jesus had been dealing with the people all day, but there came a time when He said enough for this day, let us cross over to a quiet place, a place to rest. This speaks volumes because around 2008 I started to feel like God was inviting me to cross over to another place.

I didn't fully understand the process, therefore, I was going with the flow. I started attending a church in Houston, Texas called Grace. It was a large multicultural church that was led by two Caucasian brothers. I was somewhat reluctant at first but the more I went the more I liked it. One day the church announced that they were doing baptisms and I signed up. This was my opportunity to release the years of baggage I had been carrying.

All I could think about was leaving my past in the water and coming up a new woman with a blessed future in Christ. In March 2008 I showed up to service with a made up mind. This was for me and God to reconnect on a whole new level.

I will never forget; we had a guest soloist that day by the name of Micah Stampley. Before the baptisms he sung "Alpha and Omega" by Israel Houghton and this sparked a fire in my soul. As I stood there, I could feel the power of the Holy Spirit shifting some things in my life.

I found myself worshipping Him from a place I hadn't worshiped before. God was preparing me for healing and the manifestation of His blessings. In that moment He was "bridging the gap" between my pain and my purpose. I could feel His unwavering love and His great sacrifice for me. I didn't want to be anywhere else but in His presence. This was my set time. When the time came for me to go down into the water, I knew that my life would never be the same.

When I came up out of the water, I couldn't help but notice how refreshed I felt. Consciously I felt like a brand new woman, but it wasn't soon after that the enemy would come to try me. The difference this time is that I wasn't going to respond how I had in the past. I wanted something new and I was determined to find it. God had a purpose for creating me, but the enemy worked overtime in my life to ensure that I never found out what that purpose was.

He sent many into my life to throw me off course, but God kept me through it all. I experienced weapons of mass destruction in my life. The hardships and trials that were thrust upon me should have taken me out, especially that dysfunctional marriage, but God continued to give me the strength to persevere. What I endured would have killed someone else or made them take their own life, but God!

I spent many years thinking I was stuck in a rut, but God had a plan. I questioned myself for an awfully long time wondering what my purpose was. I didn't feel like I had a purpose. I'm a natural giver, but I knew that I was put here on earth to be more than a giver. One day I was talking to the publisher about a different project that God had given me for a dear friend. She asked if she could pray for me and I said yes.

During the prayer she said, "God is bridging the gap between your pain and your purpose!" We both started screaming and she said, "that is a book title" and I agreed. I didn't waste any time setting this assignment in motion because I knew that God was saying not only was He bridging the gap for me, but I would help bridge the gap for others through my testimony.

The parts of me that were left empty and exposed by the selfishness of man was being filled and covered by the blood of Jesus. I could never get to the other side of the bridge because I kept falling through the cracks. Jesus became the cracks and in due time I was able to finally transition to the other side. I was finally able to experience the peace, joy, happiness, love, comfort, and success that had been calling out to me for many years.

Only God could take my pain and purpose, infuse them together and use them for His glory. If it were up to me, I would probably still be stuck on stupid in a failing marriage because I didn't see anything else for my future. 1st John 4:4 says, "Greater is He (God) who is in us, than he (satan) that is in the world." Since God lives in us there is nothing we can't overcome. You and I do not have to live defeated lives.

No matter where you are in your life right now, God can cause you to bridge the gap between your pain and your purpose. He is no respecter of person. If He did it for me, He can and will do it for you. There is no trial or obstacle that is too hard for God. He knows who you are, but you must know WHOSE you are. That was my biggest issue, not knowing who I was based on the word of God because I hadn't been taught that. I was basing the sole purpose of my life off the words spoken by my parents and others. Let me encourage you today to know that you are fearfully and wonderfully made in the image and likeness of God.

You don't have to settle for anything less than Jesus and His righteousness. I'm not saying that every day will be peaches and cream, but I am saying that life is much easier with God in it than with Him out of it. John 16:33 says, "I have told you these things, so that in Me you may have peace. In this world you will have trouble but take heart for I have overcome the world."

I love this scripture! God never said we wouldn't encounter things in this life. He said we would face trials and tribulations because of the sin that entered the world through the disobedience of man. I thank God for Jesus who died and rose again so He could take authority over the enemy and his deceptive ways.

The end of the quote I used in the beginning of this chapter says, "A healed person understands that the actions of others has absolutely nothing to do with them. Each day you get to decide which one you will be." I made the decision to be the healed woman that God created me to be. Through this book God was working on the inner while preparing my heart for an outer display of love and affection towards those who had hurt me in the past. One of those being my father.

Not long after completing the book I was led to have a discussion with my father. I must admit I was somewhat leery and didn't know what the outcome would be, but God knew. During the discussion with my father, I disclosed that I was writing a book about my childhood, and he said, "I know I am the villain, but all I ask is that you tell the truth!

"Tell the truth!"

When my father spoke those words, they ignited a new flame in me that caused me to go back and truly ponder the things I witnessed verses the things I was told. It dawned on me that I could have been upset with him about things that were never said or never happened. The healed version of myself was able to finally take lemons and make some thirst quenching lemonade, because I felt fulfilled after talking to my father. I was able to see him as the hero dad I remembered as a little girl.

The funny thing about this is, it only happened because I made a choice to no longer make his stuff about me. I decided to become healed and whole and God has done the rest. The word says that I will become what I think about and purpose in my heart.

Today, we must understand that in order to live life on purpose, we must be intentional about letting others off the hook. We must walk, talk, live, breath, and eat forgiveness. People are going to be people and many times that will come with offense, but when we learn that their issues are about them and not us our lives will flourish.

I had a choice to choose life and that more abundantly, because the cost had already been paid. I was living my life as a slave when I was made free. You are free today! Today is your day to claim the victory over your adversity and to walk out of the land of bondage, over the bridge of pain, and into your life filled with purpose and power.

Bridging The Gap Between Pain and Purpose

Let Us Pray!

~~~~~~~~~~~~~~~~~~~~~~~~~~~~~~~~~~

Father, in the mighty name of Jesus, I thank you for this opportunity to come before your throne of mercy and grace.

Father, please forgive me of my sins and allow Your will to be done on earth as it is in heaven in my life.

Father, I have been rejected, abused, mistreated, neglected, disappointed, lied on, talked about, and abandoned. (Add the other things that apply to you)

Father, I ask today that you forgive me for harboring any unforgiveness and bitterness.

Father forgive me for operating in fear and not faith.

Father, I ask this day that You cleanse me of all unrighteousness and that you heal me from all pain. Father cleanse me and renew a right spirit within me.

Father, you bridge the gap between my pain and my purpose through the shed blood of Jesus Christ.

Father, I want to be more like you, walking in love, joy, mercy, grace, and compassion.

Father, I thank you today for making all things new in my life for today I surrender the will of the old man.

Father raise me up and allow me to stand against the wiles of the enemy.

Father, I thank you that the enemy is defeated in my life and I have the victory through Jesus Christ.

Father, I bless, praise, and magnify Your holy name. In Jesus Name Amen!

Author Bio
~Yulanda Braxton~

Yulanda is known for her alluring smile that warms the heart of every person she meets.

Yulanda loves the Lord and has dedicated her life to being a kingdom representative.

Yulanda has worked in the automotive industry for twenty plus years and she is also the owner of Stellar Landscaping Services and YB Stellar Group.

Yulanda lives with her husband and their dog, Job. In her free time, she loves serving at her church, helping the needy, reading, and traveling.